THE YELLOW KITE

Story Arlene Blanchard
Pictures Tony Wells

Published by Dinosaur Publications

Today is Toby's birthday.
On his chair is a large parcel
tied with yellow ribbon.
"I wonder what it is?" says Toby.

"Look!"
Toby tears off the
wrapping paper and
there is a big yellow kite.
"Let's go to the park
and fly it after we've
had tea."

A big gust of wind
carries Toby's kite
high up into the sky.

"What an exciting birthday it's been," says Toby to his friends, as three of them snuggle up under the bedclothes.

"Hold on to my kite,"
yells Toby, suddenly.
"It's trying to fly away."

"There's the moon with
a long cord tied to its nose,"
says Toby, pointing.
"It's just like my kite."

"Would you like to come down
and have tea with me?"
called a voice below them.
"Yes, please," shout the
four friends all together.

"Well, slide down the cord
and I'll put the kettle on."
The old man ties the end of
his cord round a heavy stone.

"Would you like a sugar cake?"
asks the old man.
The four friends nod excitedly
as the old man plucks a handful
of sugar stars out of the sky
and gives them two each.

"Please come and visit me again.
I am the moon-kite man and
you'll find me here every night."
"Thank you, we will,"
says Toby and his friends.

"Did we really go and
see the moon-kite man,"
asks Toby, "or were
we dreaming?"
The four friends look
at each other, wondering
which it was.

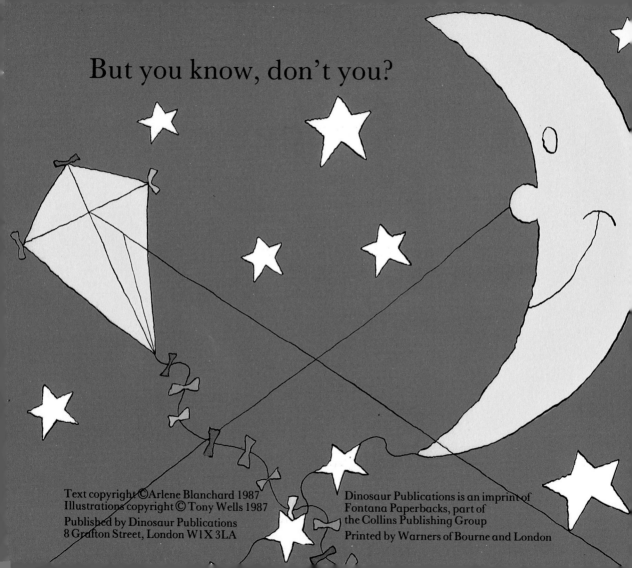

But you know, don't you?

Published by Dinosaur Publications
8 Grafton Street, London W1X 3LA

Dinosaur Publications is an imprint of
Fontana Paperbacks, part of
the Collins Publishing Group

Printed by Warners of Bourne and London